Rr

Bela Davis

Abdo
THE ALPHABET
Kids

abdopublishing.com

Published by Abdo Kids, a division of ABDO, PO Box 398166, Minneapolis, Minnesota 55439.
Copyright © 2017 by Abdo Consulting Group, Inc. International copyrights reserved in all countries.
No part of this book may be reproduced in any form without written permission from the publisher.

Printed in the United States of America, North Mankato, Minnesota.

102016
012017

 THIS BOOK CONTAINS
RECYCLED MATERIALS

Photo Credits: iStock, Shutterstock

Production Contributors: Teddy Borth, Jennie Forsberg, Grace Hansen

Design Contributors: Christina Doffing, Candice Keimig, Dorothy Toth

Publisher's Cataloging in Publication Data

Names: Davis, Bela, author.

Title: Rr / by Bela Davis.

Description: Minneapolis, Minnesota : Abdo Kids, 2017 | Series: The alphabet |
    Includes bibliographical references and index.

Identifiers: LCCN 2016943898 | ISBN 9781680808940 (lib. bdg.) |
    ISBN 9781680796049 (ebook) | ISBN 9781680796711 (Read-to-me ebook)

Subjects: LCSH: English language--Alphabet--Juvenile literature. | Alphabet
    books--Juvenile literature.

Classification: DDC 421/.1--dc23

LC record available at http://lccn.loc.gov/2016943898

Table of Contents

Rr

Ruby **r**ides a **r**olle**r** coaste**r**.

Rr

Ryan **r**ows down the **r**ive**r**.

Rr

Rachel **relaxes** on a **r**ing.

9

Rr

Rob **controls** a **r**eally big robot.

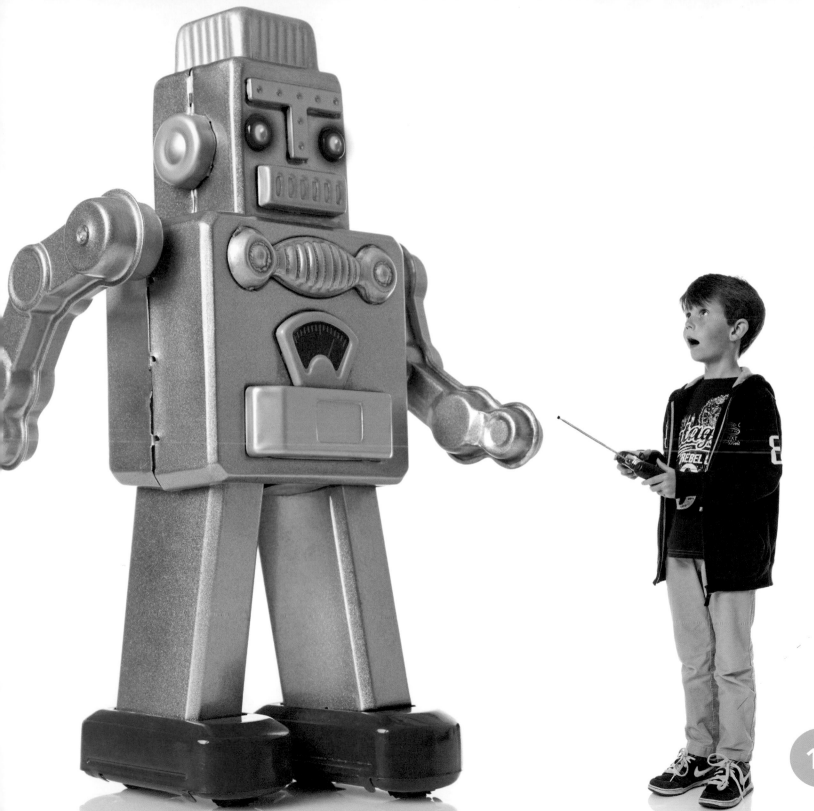

Rr

Ricky **r**uns in the **r**ain.

Rr

Riley **r**ides a horse.

Rr

Rocco feeds a **r**abbit.

Rr

Ruth **r**aises he**r** **r**ight a**r**m.

Rr

What is **R**ose doing?

(**r**eading)

More **Rr** Words

raccoon

raspberry

rake

rocket

Glossary

control
to cause something to act or function in a certain way.

relax
to spend time resting or doing something enjoyable.

Index

abdokids.com

Use this code to log on to abdokids.com and access crafts, games, videos, and more!

Abdo Kids Code:
TRK8940

24